LET'S-READ-AND-FIND-OUT SCIENCE®

STAGE 1

Snow Is Falling

by Franklyn M. Branley • illustrated by Holly Keller

HarperCollins Publishers

With special thanks to Chris Strong of the
National Weather Service for his expert advice.

The *Let's-Read-and-Find-Out Science* book series was originated by Dr. Franklyn M. Branley, Astronomer Emeritus and former Chairman of the American Museum–Hayden Planetarium, and was formerly co-edited by him and Dr. Roma Gans, Professor Emeritus of Childhood Education, Teachers College, Columbia University. Text and illustrations for each of the books in the series are checked for accuracy by an expert in the relevant field. For more information about Let's-Read-and-Find-Out Science books, write to HarperCollins Children's Books, 10 East 53rd Street, New York, NY 10022.

HarperCollins®, 🐾®, and Let's Read-and-Find-Out Science® are trademarks of HarperCollins Publishers Inc.

Snow Is Falling
For information address HarperCollins Children's Books, a division of HarperCollins Publishers,
10 East 53rd Street, New York, NY 10022. http://www.harperchildrens.com

Library of Congress Cataloging-in-Publication Data
Branley, Franklyn Mansfield, 1915–
   Snow is falling / Franklyn M. Branley ; illustrated by Holly Keller.
      p.   cm. — (Let's-read-and-find-out science. Stage 1)
   Summary: Describes snow's physical qualities and how quantities of it can be fun as well as dangerous.
   ISBN 0-06-027990-7. — ISBN 0-06-027991-5 (lib. bdg.). — ISBN 0-06-445186 0 (pbk.)
   1. Snow—Juvenile literature.   [1. Snow.]   I. Keller, Holly, ill. II. Title. III. Series.
QC926.37.B7   1999
551.57'84—dc21

98-23106
CIP
AC

Typography by Elynn Cohen
9   10
❖
Revised Edition
Originally published in 1963

Snow Is Falling

Night has come and snow is falling. It is quiet. The snow falls without a sound. Look at the streetlight. The snow is falling in front of it. It may fall all night.

5

The snow may fall all day. The snow gets deeper and deeper. Lawns are white. Trees are white, and so are the roofs of houses. Everything is covered. Everything is white. Everything is quiet and cold.

It is always cold when snow falls. It is so cold that
water vapor freezes in the air. This makes snowflakes.
Let a snowflake fall on your mitten.

Sometimes snowflakes stick together and fall as a cluster of flakes. They also fall as single flakes. Look at the single snowflake on your mitten. Use your magnifying glass to make it look bigger. Each snowflake has six sides.

The snowflake may look like this

or this,

or like this.

9

Sometimes snow is wet and sticky. When you walk in wet, sticky snow, you splash, and slip, and slide. Sometimes snow is light, dry, and fluffy. Walking through light snow is fun. You can kick it into the air. You can scoop up a big shovelful of light, dry snow.

You can run and roll and ski in the snow. You can slide on your sled. You can build a snowman.

Snow can be fun, but what does snow do? Is it good for plants? Is it good for animals? Is it good for you and me? Let's find out.

Snow covers plants that must stay in the ground all winter. The snow is like a blanket. Because the plants are covered, wind, ice, and cold cannot hurt them. Plants that are covered with snow can live through the cold winter. Snow is good for plants.

15

Snow is good for many animals, too. Worms and mice, moles and chipmunks stay under the ground all winter. The blanket of snow keeps the wind and cold from the animals. Snow helps to keep them warm.

Get two thermometers. On a cold day when the wind is blowing, bury one thermometer in the snow. Hang the other thermometer outdoors, but not in direct sunlight.

After an hour or so, uncover the thermometer in the snow. What is the temperature? It is warmer under the snow. Snow protects many plants and animals from wind and from getting very cold.

Snow protects people, too. In the far north, people sometimes built houses of snow. They built a house from blocks cut out of hard, packed snow. They piled blocks high to make a round snow house. Sometimes people today still build houses like this.

Snow is good in other ways. Melted snow gives us water for our wells, our streams, and our rivers.

When winter is over, the sun warms the snow.

The snow melts slowly, and water goes into the soil. The soil is ready for planting. Plants grow well in the loose, moist, warm soil.

Sometimes snow is not good. When strong winds blow, the soft, quiet snow becomes a howling blizzard. A blizzard makes life hard for animals and people.

When snow piles high, it may be so
deep that animals cannot move. The snow
covers their food. Power lines blow down. Cars get stuck.

The deep snows of winter may melt fast in the spring. Sometimes there is more water than streams can carry, so the streams overflow. Houses, barns, and whole towns are flooded.

Snow can make life hard. But it also makes it fun to roll, run, ski, and slide.

Snow gives us water for wells, streams, and rivers.
Snow is good for plants and animals. Snow is good
for people. It is good for you and me.

TWO SNOW EXPERIMENTS TO TRY

- Does it matter what color your jacket is when you're playing in the snow? Try this experiment to see. You will need: a piece of white cloth, a piece of black cloth, and two thermometers. (The pieces of cloth should be the same thickness.) Make sure the reading on both thermometers is the same. Put the thermometers in a sunny place in the snow. Cover one thermometer with the white cloth and the other with the black cloth. Wait ten minutes. Read the temperature on each thermometer. Cover the thermometers again. Wait another ten minutes and read the temperature again. Which thermometer has the higher temperature? Which color jacket would keep you warmer if you went skiing or sledding on a sunny day?

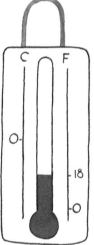

- During winter, people put salt on icy roads and sidewalks to help make the ice melt. You can watch this work in your own kitchen. You will need: a tray of ice cubes, two bowls, and some salt. Put the same number of ice cubes in each bowl. In one of the bowls, stir in some salt. Watch the bowls for fifteen minutes, stirring them often. In which bowl are the ice cubes melting more quickly?

SNOW WEB SITES TO VISIT

You can explore the following web sites to learn more about snow and snowy-day activities:

www.nws.noaa.gov
  The National Weather Service page has links to hundreds of weather-related sites.

www.crh.noaa.gov/mkx/owlie/owlie.htm
  This web site has safety tips for winter storms and blizzards.

www.npac.syr.edu/textbook/kidsweb/Sciences/weather.html
  Learn about environmental science, weather, and geology with this web site.

ENJOY THESE BOOKS ABOUT SNOW:

THE SNOWY DAY by Ezra Jack Keats
THE BIG SNOW by Berta and Elmer Hader
THE FIRST SNOWFALL by Anne Rockwell